For information, address:
National Society of Tole and Decorative Painters, Inc.
P.O. Box 808
Newton, Kansas 67114

Printed in the U.S.A. by
Trafton & Autry Printers, Inc.
Amarillo, Texas

ISBN 0-943883-15-6

HOMES FOR THE HOLIDAYS

WITH PAINTED TREASURES

By Mary Jo Leisure and Margy Wentz

Photography by Wyatt McSpadden

Published by The National Society of Tole & Decorative Painters, Inc., Newton, Kansas

Lo! Now are come the holidays,
  Let everyone be jolly.
We've decorated every home,
  With candlelight and holly.

Remember Christmas everyone,
  And celebrate with cheer.
We've painted special treasures now,
  To share throughout the year.

For Christmas is a special time,
  When family gathers round,
And friends share joy and cheerfulness,
  And loving deeds abound.

4

HOMES FOR THE HOLIDAYS

WITH PAINTED TREASURES

Homes and holidays — the two words mingle naturally. Both speak of remembering, of decorating, of celebrating, of sharing and of loving. There is in the holidays the unique opportunity for expression of the traditions that make the home special. There is in the home the possibility of creating days of beauty to be cherished and remembered.

Homes are transformed by the holidays. Holidays allow us to turn dull, ordinary, repetitive days into magical, mystical times. For the holidays, we add distinctive decorative touches to our homes to create an atmosphere of excitement and celebration.

Of all the days of celebration, none stir the emotions, senses, and memories like Christmas. No other holiday is as eagerly awaited, thoroughly celebrated, and dearly cherished. There are unlimited possibilities in Christmas.

Christmas is a shining season that invites us to create the extraordinary in our homes. By planning special details and decorations for the holidays, and making our homes as beautiful as possible, we bring grace to our homes for the holidays. By creating and displaying hand painted treasures we can transform the holidays and bring distinction to the home and invite warm memories for years to come. Our homes made beautiful and inviting for the holidays enrich us, and encourage the spirit of loving and sharing.

Our Christmas wish is that in sharing this volume, you will be inspired through visual example, to create the beauty of Christmas in your homes for the holidays.

ˈENTS

REMEMBERING

Sing we all merrily,
Christmas is here.
The day we remember
all through the year.
Traditional Verse

$\mathcal{C}$hristmas is remembering . . .
the traditions, decorations, and toys of childhood,
the nostalgic aroma of gingerbread and pies baking,
the warmth of family bathed in candlelight,
the holly and the holy.

Observance of Christmas is both secular and sacred. For those whose faith is central to the celebration, the essence of Christmas is in the remembrance of the Christ Child.

Country and Christmas are as natural companions as Santa and Uncle Sam. Decorations that blend the spirit of the season with patriotic pride evoke nostalgic memories.

$\mathscr{R}$ecollections of Christmas past are inevitable in this room transformed for the holidays. Skillful attention to detail creates a special look – placement of the holiday tree so that it is reflected in the corner mirror, the use of the Christmas rose on the fireplace screen, mantle and tree, and the subtle repetition throughout the decorations of the colors used in the stenciling and faux finish.

This room, with its stockings which are hung by the chimney with care, will call up special memories for Christmases to come.

17

Christmas is a sentimental season, a quiet time for reflection and for remembering family, including those who will not again share the holidays.

While cold winter may bring
    snow,
  Inside we're warmed by fireside
    glow.
  Santa comes with each December
  Christmas time we long remember.

DECORATING

Christmas is coming.
Let's decorate all,
With candles and ornaments
Throughout the hall.
Traditional Verse

$\mathcal{C}$hristmas is decorating.

We measure the very approach of the holiday with the often asked question, "Have you decorated yet?" Like no other time of the year, the Christmas season provides unlimited opportunities for decorative expression.

Flourishes of greenery, swags of ribbon, and glowing lights combine with painted treasures to build a mood, evoke a memory, and create a tradition.

27

Christmas is a theme which the creative decorator can play with timeless variations – drawing on traditional motifs such as trees, ornaments, soldiers, bells, angels, wreaths, santas, and stockings.

*H*and painted decorations created today, like the heirlooms of Christmas past, become the treasured keepsakes of tomorrow.

*S*antas, sleds, and soldiers seem to shine.

The Christmas tree, with varied and wondrous ornaments, is the centerpiece of Christmas decorating.

$\mathcal{R}$ing out, oh bells, on Christmas day.

*A*ngels – beautiful, lovely, smiling, heavenly messengers – bring Christmas tidings.

$\mathcal{W}$reaths are versatile embellishments for the holiday home, decorating interior spaces over the mantelpiece, table or buffet, and beckoning a holiday welcome at the front door.

*S*anta is everything that is Christmas – ancient, new, jolly, caring, giving, sharing.

*I*n summer sun,
  In winter snow,
  A dress of green
  You always show.
  O Christmas Tree
  O Christmas Tree
  How lovely are
  Your branches.
    Old English variation of "O Tannenbaum"

EBRATING

At Christmas be joyful and all celebrate;
Give cheer to your friends,
The small with the great.
At Christmas be merry and thankful withal;
And welcome your neighbors,
The great with the small.
Traditional Verse

Christmas is celebrating, with fine food, family and friends. Once the tree is trimmed, the house is dressed and the table set, you'll be ready to welcome friends to your home to share the warmth of the season and celebrate.

We look forward to Christmas
January through November
And enjoy celebrating
All throughout December.

*H*olidays allow us to interrupt a series of ordinary days, and brighten our homes and lives with extraordinary days. Christmas provides opportunities to create and appreciate beauty, to add decorative distinctiveness, and to enjoy celebrative moments.

There is unlimited opportunity for self-expression and pleasure in
Christmas. It is a special time to be cherished, not neglected
nor taken lightly. Small details handled lovingly and with
thoughtfulness contribute to the spirit of celebration. Prisms of
light on gleaming crystal, a magnificent array of rich reds and
shimmering golds, shadows cast on the walls by the shutters,
and lovingly wrapped gifts at each place bring grace to this
home for the holidays.

*H*oliday paintings grace the table.

*R*ichly polished wood, gleaming silver, and glistening crystal glow in flickering candlelight.

The decorations done, the house graced
with guests, merry music mingles
melodiously with laughter.

Christmas celebrates the senses . . .
Christmas carols sung and heard,
Shining gifts with ribbons curl'd
Winter frost and ice and snow,
Crackling logs and firelight glow,
But most of all fresh cookies baking,
And homemade goodies in the making.

As important as the ornaments and trees are the delicious treats that celebrate the season.

*C*hristmas spirit mingles
with star spangled patriotism to
celebrate an American Christmas.

$\mathcal{A}$ Santa celebration!

The snow lies white on roof and tree,
    Frost fairies creep about,
The world's as still as it can be
    And Santa Claus is out.

He's making haste his gifts to leave,
    While the stars show his way,
There'll soon be no more Christmas Eve
    Tomorrow's Christmas Day!
                    Anonymous

With evergreen branches our walls we array,
To celebrate Christmas, our high holiday.

SHARING

*Somehow not only for Christmas,
but all the long year through,
The joy that you share with others,
is the joy that comes back to you.*

Traditional Verse

*C*hristmas is sharing . . .
Joyfully decorated homes,
Festively prepared food,
Lovingly handcrafted gifts.
Our faith, hopes, and dreams.

*T*he sharing of Christmas comes
naturally to those who create
their own specially prepared
foods, decorations and presents,
for gifts from the hands are
gifts from the heart.

The essence of Christmas for
decorative painters is sharing
with family, neighbors and
friends, gifts that have been
creatively painted. Such gifts
will be enjoyed not only today,
but as the years go by will become treasured reminders of
Christmas past.

$\mathcal{S}$haring doubles
joy and diminishes
sorrow.

91

*S*haring gifts is a collaborative
adventure, requiring someone to
give and someone to receive.

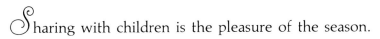

Sharing with children is the pleasure of the season.

*M*ay joy come from God above,
To all who share their Christmas love.
13th Century Verse

LOVING

Love came down at Christmas,
Love all lovely, Love Divine.
Love was born at Christmas.
Stars and Angels gave the sign.
Christina Rossetti

A little child,
A shining star.
A stable rude,
The door ajar.

Yet in that place,
So crude, forlorn,
The hope of all
The world was born.
Anonymous

$\mathcal{C}$hristmas is loving . . .
the loving gift of the Christ Child,
the loving devotion of family,
the loving affection of friends.

$\mathcal{F}$or Christians, Christmas is the celebration of the birth of the Baby in the stable in Bethlehem, nearly two thousand years ago. But whatever your faith, the spirit of Christmas is love.

Homes made beautiful for the holidays are of an infinite loveliness. One of the saddest things in life is the loss of opportunity; but with small acts of care and kindness, you can thoughtfully create an atmosphere of love that will enrich the lives of those who enter your home for the holidays.

When love and skill
work together, expect a
masterpiece.
John Ruskin.

$\mathcal{L}$o! How a rose e're blooming,
From tender stem hath sprung.
Of Jesse's lineage coming.
As those of old hath sung.

This flower, whose fragrance tender,
With sweetness fills the air,
Dispels with glorious splendor,
The darkness everywhere.
Traditional Carole

Modern life can be as threatening as was medieval; we, too, should make winter solstice rituals — lovingly light candles, lamps and fires to add gaiety and warmth to the dark days of the year that provide the setting for Christmas.

$\mathcal{S}$urrounded by winter's beauty, and cheered by cozy fire, warm messages of concern and affection are carefully prepared. Christmas cards are one of the most thoughtful aspects of Christmas, sending messages of love and caring.

"Let all that you do be done in love."

*E*njoy a heavenly holiday in your home this Christmas.

$\mathcal{W}$e've celebrated Christmas
    With peace and love to men.
        And every year
        With hearty cheer,
    We'll celebrate again.

IRECTORY OF

HOMES

$\mathcal{C}$hristmas is a holiday very dear to the hearts of members of the Society of Decorative Painters. Each year members of the chapters of the Society engage in a wide variety of Christmas projects, such as decorating ornaments and trees for various charities. Four of the past six years, the invitation has gone to all members of the Society to paint ornaments for a distinctive decorative painting tree for the Trees of Christmas exhibit at the Smithsonian Institution.

Examples of such ornaments are displayed on the wreath on the opposite page and on this page. These charming examples of decorative painting were crafted by Certified Decorative Artists of the Society of Decorative Painters. The wreath was lovingly created by Aileen Bratton of Albuquerque, New Mexico, President of the Society.

The wreath is displayed in the offices of the Society in Newton, Kansas, along with many other items belonging to the Society and to the Decorative Arts Collection, Inc.

The Decorative Arts Collection, Inc. is a corporation created for the purpose of collecting, preserving, and displaying decorative art.

The Society of Decorative Painters, whose official name is The National Society of Tole and Decorative Painters, Inc., is a membership association that has as its primary purpose to stimulate interest in and appreciation for the art of tole and decorative painting.

Inquiries about either corporation may be addressed to P.O. Box 808, Newton, Kansas 67114.